THE WEATHER IN JAPAN

MICHAEL LONGLEY

The Weather
in Japan

Wake Forest University Press

Wake Forest University Press
This book is for sale only in North
America. Copyright © Michael Longley
First U.S. edition published 2000

For permission, required to reprint or
broadcast more than several lines, write to:
Wake Forest University Press
Post Office Box 7333,Winston-Salem,
NC 27109

Printed in the United States by
Thomson-Shore. Text set in Bembo type
L.C. Catalogue Card no. 00-130157
ISBN 0-916390-95-0 (paperback)
ISBN 0-916390-96-9 (cloth)

For Ronald Ewart

In my ideal village the houses lie scattered
Over miles and are called a townland, while in yours
Neighbours live above and below, and a nightcap
Means climbing up steps in the direction of the stars.

CONTENTS

Latches click softly in the trees
James Wright

WATER-BURN

We should have been galloping on horses, their hoofprints
Splashes of light, divots kicked out of the darkness,
Or hauling up lobster pots in a wake of sparks. Where
Were the otters and seals? Were the dolphins on fire?
Yes, we should have been doing more with our lives.

PALE BUTTERWORT

Pale butterwort's smoky blue colours your eyes:
I thought of this when I tried to put together
Your every feature, but a buzzard distracted me
As it quartered the tree-tops and added its skraik
Or screel to the papery purr of the dragonflies'
Love-flight, and with so much happening overhead
I forgot the pale butterwort there on the ground
Spreading its leaves like a starfish and digesting
Insects that squirm on each adhesive tongue and
Feed the terror in your eyes, your smoky blue eyes.

THE LAPWING

Carrigskeewaun in May light has unsettled me.
Each butterwort flourishes an undertaker's lamp
For the poisoned swan unfolding on David's pond
Like a paper flower in a saucer. 'Milkwort,'
I mumble to the piss-scattering wind. 'Why me?'
The lapwing replies and falters like a bi-plane
Above her nest. 'Why me?' The lapwing and I
Watch over each other and we speak in tongues.

THE COMBER

A moment before the comber turns into
A breaker – sea-spray, raggedy rainbows –
Water and sunlight contain all the colours
And suspend between Inishbofin and me
The otter, and thus we meet, without my scent
In her nostrils, the uproar of my presence,
My unforgivable shadow on the sand –
Even if this is the only sound I make.

THE METEORITE

We crossed the fields by moonlight and by moonlight
Counted the whooper swans, each a white silhouette,
A shape from Iceland, and picked out thirty, was it,
Before we were interrupted by the meteorite
And its reflection that among the swans was lit.

THE EXCAVATOR

An excavator at Carrigskeewaun is digging
Near the duach, between the lakes, no more than
More space for water and waterbirds, a pond
For you and me to look at from the double-bed.
Imagine a kestrel stooping to tipple there.

THE FLOCK

I am touching your shoulder and pointing out the seals
Head and shoulders above seal-grey water, hand-swimmers
Who look towards us before they fold shimmery cheeks
Into the ripples and disappear. Are they mating,
We wonder. Or suckling their pups. Or just playing.

Touching your shoulder for a second longer takes me
Below the surface, and there I move among the seals
Without frightening them, a shepherd among his sheep
Going over them all and counting his flock by fives
And rescuing one lamb from the seaweedy tangle.

THE SEAL

Will you remember how we watched the minute hand
Move between two cupids, gilded wings underneath
The Wave by Gustave Courbet, so strong a swimmer
He was nicknamed 'the seal' by local fishermen,

Or how in Chardin's *Vase of Flowers* – tuberoses,
Sweetpeas and carnations, his only surviving flower
Piece – the Chinese vase reflects a window and three
Or four petals have just fallen on to the table?

A TOUCH
after the Irish

she is the touch of pink
on crab apple blossom
and hawthorn and she melts
frost flowers with her finger

NIGHT TIME

Without moonlight or starlight we forgot about love
As we joined the blind ewe and the unsteady horses.

THE WEATHER IN JAPAN

Makes bead curtains of the rain,
Of the mist a paper screen.

THE WELL AT TULLY
for Nicholas Harmon

I

Looking into the well at Tully, the soul of your estate, I
Nearly tell you that 'come home' in Scots can mean 'be born',
That the Incarnation explains itself in wet fields like these.

Lichens inhale the Mayo weather and make the branches
Lacy on trees your mother grew from apple pips, Irish
Peach, russets and bramleys, blushes that seep through skins.

II

This view of the river from a window-seat attracts you
Like a sea trout, though the Bunowen will turn housebreaker
Lifting the rugs, lapping the tables and chairs, calling up

The lone English sergeant in charge of dykes and bridges,
Formal in red coat and stripes, but from the navel down
Buck-naked, immune to assassination or ridicule –

A legend, as one day the strongest man for miles around
(And the townland's only Protestant) will be, who helps you
Manhandle like an Inca handbarrow-loads of boulders

Onto the scraw-fence, as though you were creating the first
Windbreak in history, where I hunker in November rain
And eavesdrop: 'I'm nineteen stone, and two of them is fat!'

III

Reflections of all who have taken a drink of water here
On hands and knees should linger in the well at Tully
And be given their place indoors, out of the wind and rain.

You are right to carry to your kitchen across the fields
Buckets of spring water, ice-cold always and good as new
Thanks to the caretaker frog in that ferny interior.

BURREN PRAYER

Gentians and lady's bedstraw embroider her frock.
Her pockets are full of sloes and juniper berries.

Quaking-grass panicles monitor her heartbeat.
Her reflection blooms like mudwort in a puddle.

Sea lavender and Irish eyebright at Poll Salach,
On Black Head saxifrage and mountain-everlasting.

Our Lady of the Fertile Rocks, protect the Burren.
Protect the Burren, Our Lady of the Fertile Rocks.

A SPRIG OF BAY

in memory of Sean Dunne, 1956–95

I

Stepping among recent windfalls and couch grass
Like wet raffia unravelling and beech seedlings,
I glimpse this rundown orchard's original plan
In the lofty bay tree and the well it canopies,

And drink spring water to your memory and pick
Leaves for the dried beans in your Cork bedsit
As you appear out of those long-haired bearded days
To accept, Sean, cook and poet, a sprig of bay.

II

I wish I could introduce you to this friend of mine
Who is rebuilding a ruined flax mill as a ruin
– If it is a flax mill, or a mill for grinding wheat
(A millstone leans against the wall) – no matter what,

You walk away from the rainy fields into a rainy
Room, windows that let the winds come in, a chimney
That opens up to a square of sky and ivy. Sean,
Wear like a gigantic bangle the cracked millstone.

III

In the abandoned schoolhouse I shelter from the rain
With hundreds of pupils and look beyond boreen
And hollow bog (the 'spother' in these parts) to where
The last turf was stacked for Old Head and the hookers,

And I imagine you, Sean, as in a game of hide
And seek covering, uncovering the eyes of childhood,
Or else, absent because you laboured through the night,
You are the boy who snoozes on the last turf-cart.

THE FACTORY
for Brendan Kennelly

I open a can of peas and I open up
That factory, balancing on tons of pea-vines
And forking them out of the sky into machines,
Millions of peas on a white conveyor belt, sleepy
Eyes, surfacing from a vat sunk into the floor
A gigantic iron shopping-basket full of cans.

The only student-slave able for hard labour,
Kennelly helps me assemble my rusty bed
In a Nissen hut in the middle of vague England,
And create out of cardboard boxes a mattress,
There to collapse, aching, blistery, and waken
At dawn to a blackbird on the corrugated iron,

Kennelly's voice, long before children and wives
Helping me feel at home amid the productive
Cacophony, cans spiralling down from the roof –
Already the tubby, rollicking, broken Christ
Talking too much, drowning me in his hurlygush
Which makes the sound water makes over stones.

DAMIANA
from the Latin

Forget about Damiana, Rome's one and only
Self-appointed hermaphrodite poet/poetess,
Too lily-livered to publish but blasting others,
Especially the girls – Sulpicia, for instance,
Amorous elegist supreme – taunting Tibullus,
Poetry's true lover among cassia and roses,
Jeering at Propertius's desperate intensity,
Taking the piss out of schoolmasterly Macer
For poems about ornithology and snake bites –
Yes, shooting at song birds while plugging himself/
Herself, his/her name derived from the dried leaves
Of *Turnera diffusa* – damiana – a quack
Medicament for spleen, club-footed iambics,
Blocked bowels, and even sexual impotence.

HEARTSEASE

When Helen, destroyer of cities, destroyer of men,
Slipped the lads a Mickey Finn of wine and heartsease,
Unhappiness's cure, a painkiller strong enough
To keep you dry-eyed for a day even if mummy
Or daddy pegs out, or your brother or son's bumped off
On the doorstep in front of you (an Egyptian drug?),
She hadn't a clue that where I hail from – beyond
The north wind, Hyperborean, or nearly – heartsease
Is kiss-me-quick, kiss-me-behind-the-garden-gate,
That in Donegal this pansy gets mixed up with selfheal.

THE PARODY

If dandering three times around the wooden
Horse, groping the carpentry for a knothole and
Imitating the voices of absent wives, Helen
Had impersonated you, sillier than Diomedes
Would I have fallen for the parody, cried out
And turned death and destruction inside out?

IN THE ILIAD

When I was left alone with our first-born
She turned in the small hours her hungry face
To my diddy and tried to suck that button.
Her spittle condenses on my grey hairs.

We wear them like medals for our children
And even in nakedness look overdressed.
In the *Iliad* spears go through them and,
Later, one's ripped from Agamemnon's chest.

THE VISION OF THEOCLYMENUS

What class of a nightmare are you living through,
Poor bastards, your faces, knees shrouded in darkness,
The atmosphere electric with keening – for it all
Ends in tears – the walls bloody, and the crossbeams
Like branches after a cloudburst drippling blood,
The porch full of zombies, likewise the haggard
Where they jostle to go underground, and no
Sun while deadly marsh-gas envelops the globe?

Though it feels to me like midnight here, I'm not,
As you say, peerie-heedit, in need of help –
With my eyes, ears and two feet, with unimpaired
Intelligence I shall make it through those doors
To the real world, and leave hanging over you
Catastrophe, richly deserved, inescapable.

ALL OF THESE PEOPLE

Who was it who suggested that the opposite of war
Is not so much peace as civilisation? He knew
Our assassinated Catholic greengrocer who died
At Christmas in the arms of our Methodist minister,
And our ice-cream man whose continuing requiem
Is the twenty-one flavours children have by heart.
Our cobbler mends shoes for everybody; our butcher
Blends into his best sausages leeks, garlic, honey;
Our cornershop sells everything from bread to kindling.
Who can bring peace to people who are not civilised?
All of these people, alive or dead, are civilised.

AT POLL SALACH
Easter Sunday, 1998

While I was looking for Easter snow on the hills
You showed me, like a concentration of violets
Or a fragment from some future unimagined sky,
A single spring gentian shivering at our feet.

A PRAYER

In our country they are desecrating churches.
May the rain that pours in pour into the font.
Because no snowflake ever falls in the wrong place,
May snow lie on the altar like an altar cloth.

THE EXHIBIT

I see them absentmindedly pat their naked bodies
Where waistcoat and apron pockets would have been.
The grandparents turn back and take an eternity
Rummaging in the tangled pile for their spectacles.

A LINEN HANDKERCHIEF
for Helen Lewis

Northern Bohemia's flax fields and the flax fields
Of Northern Ireland, the linen industry, brought Harry,
Trader in linen handkerchiefs, to Belfast, and then
After Terezín and widowhood and Auschwitz, you,

Odysseus as a girl, your sail a linen handkerchief
On which he embroidered and unpicked hundreds of names
All through the war, but in one corner the flowers
Encircling your initials never came undone.

A BUNCH OF ASPARAGUS

It was against the law for Jews to buy asparagus.
Only Aryan piss was allowed that whiff of compost.
I bring you a bunch held together with elastic bands.
Let us prepare melted butter, shavings of parmesan,
And make a meal out of the mouthwatering fasces.

A POPPY

When millions march into the mincing machine
An image in Homer picks out the individual
Tommy and the doughboy in his doughboy helmet:
'Lolling to one side like a poppy in a garden
Weighed down by its seed capsule and rainwater,
His head drooped under the heavy, crestfallen
Helmet' (an image Virgil steals – *lasso papavera*
Collo – and so do I), and so Gorgythion dies,
And the poppy that sheds its flower-heads in a day
Grows in one summer four hundred more, which means
Two thousand petals overlapping as though to make
A cape for the corn goddess or a soldier's soul.

When he was billeted in a ruined house in Arras
And found a hole in the wall beside his bed
And, rummaging inside, his hand rested on *Keats*
By Edward Thomas, did Edmund Blunden unearth
A volume which 'the tall, Shelley-like figure'
Gathering up for the last time his latherbrush,
Razor, towel, comb, cardigan, cap comforter,
Water bottle, socks, gas mask, great coat, rifle
And bayonet, hurrying out of the same building
To join his men and march into battle, left
Behind him like a gift, the author's own copy?
When Thomas Hardy died his widow gave Blunden
As a memento of many visits to Max Gate
His treasured copy of Edward Thomas's *Poems*.

THE WAR GRAVES

The exhausted cathedral reaches nowhere near the sky
As though behind its buttresses wounded angels
Snooze in a halfway house of gargoyles, rainwater
By the mouthful, broken wings among pigeons' wings.

There will be no end to clearing up after the war
And only an imaginary harvest-home where once
The Germans drilled holes for dynamite, for fieldmice
To smuggle seeds and sow them inside these columns.

The headstones wipe out the horizon like a blizzard
And we can see no farther than the day they died,
As though all of them died together on the same day
And the war was that single momentous explosion.

Mothers and widows pruned these roses yesterday,
It seems, planted sweet william and mowed the lawn
After consultations with the dead, heads meeting
Over this year's seed catalogues and packets of seeds.

Around the shell holes not one poppy has appeared,
No symbolic flora, only the tiny whitish flowers
No one remembers the names of in time, brookweed
And fairy flax, say, lamb's lettuce and penny-cress.

In mine craters so vast they are called after cities
Violets thrive, as though strewn by each cataclysm
To sweeten the atmosphere and conceal death's smell
With a perfume that vanishes as soon as it is found.

At the Canadian front line permanent sandbags
And duckboards admit us to the underworld, and then
With the beavers we surface for long enough to hear
The huge lamentations of the wounded caribou.

Old pals in the visitors' book at Railway Hollow
Have scribbled 'The severest spot. The lads did well'
'We came to remember', and the woodpigeons too
Call from the wood and all the way from Accrington.

I don't know how Rifleman Parfitt, Corporal Vance,
Private Costello of the Duke of Wellingtons,
Driver Chapman, Topping, Atkinson, Duckworth,
Dorrell, Wood come to be written in my diary.

For as high as we can reach we touch-read the names
Of the disappeared, and shut our eyes and listen to
Finches' chitters and a blackbird's apprehensive cry
Accompanying Charles Sorley's monumental sonnet.

We describe the comet at Edward Thomas's grave
And, because he was a fisherman, that headlong
Motionless deflection looks like a fisherman's fly,
Two or three white after-feathers overlapping.

Geese on sentry duty, lambs, a clattering freight train
And a village graveyard encompass Wilfred Owen's
Allotment, and there we pick from a nettle bed
One celandine each, the flower that outwits winter.

THE MOUSTACHE

The moustache Edward Thomas grew to cover up
His aesthete's features, the short-back-and-sides hair-do
That moved him to the centre of modern times, recall
My father, aged twenty, in command of a company
Who, because most of them shaved only once a week
And some not at all, were known as Longley's Babies.

THE CHOUGHS

As they ride the air currents at Six Noggins,
Rolling and soaring above the cliff face
And spreading their wing tips out like fingers,
The choughs' red claws recall my father

Telling me how the raw recruits would clutch
Their 'courting tackle' under heavy fire:
Choughs at play are the souls of young soldiers
Lifting their testicles into the sky.

JANUARY 12, 1996

He would have been a hundred today, my father,
So I write to him in the trenches and describe
How he lifts with tongs from the brazier an ember
And in its glow reads my words and sets them aside.

THE CENOTAPH

They couldn't wait to remember and improvised
A cenotaph of snow and a snowman soldier,
Inscribing 'Lest We Forget' with handfuls of stones.

THE BULLET HOLE

Imagine Uncle Matt, head full of Henryson
And Fergusson and fear of death and excitement,
After coming through the North African Campaign
Sweating it out up the steep road to Fiesole
Past the cathedral and the Roman amphitheatre,
The tombs and the temple, at the top of the hill
Turning into this road and approaching this house
And this garden where we sit with an old friend
Between peach and pomegranate trees, a pergola
And all that is left of an Etruscan wall, then
Opening fire, nervously, once, because he thinks
There are Germans in the kitchen, and leaving
In the chestnut crossbeam a hole, a stray bullet
That has taken half a century to find its mark.

DEATH OF A HORSE
after Keith Douglas

Its expression resigned, humble even, as if it knows
And doesn't mind when the man draws the first diagonal
In white across its forehead, from ear to eyeball, then
The second, death's chalky intersection, the crossroads

Where, moments before the legs stiffen and relax and
The knees give way and like water from a burst drain
The blood comes jetting out, black almost, warm and thick,
The horse goes on standing still, just staring ahead.

THE HORSES

For all of the horses butchered on the battlefield,
Shell-shocked, tripping up over their own intestines,
Drowning in the mud, the best war memorial
Is in Homer: two horses that refuse to budge
Despite threats and sweet-talk and the whistling whip,
Immovable as a tombstone, their heads drooping
In front of the streamlined motionless chariot,
Hot tears spilling from their eyelids onto the ground
Because they are still in mourning for Patroclus
Their charioteer, their shiny manes bedraggled
Under the yoke pads on either side of the yoke.

THE SEWING MACHINE

George Fleming is making out of sailors' collars
A quilt that will cover the sea bed and the graves
Of submariners in their submarines. Listen
As his sewing machine cruises among the flotsam
And picks up hundreds of waterlogged cap tallies:
Stonehenge sunk off the Nicobar Islands, *Spearfish*
And *Salmon* off Norway, *Unbeaten* and *Snapper*
In the Bay of Biscay, in the Gulf of Taranto
Tempest and *Odin* – torpedoes, depth charges,
Mines – *Pandora, Thunderbolt, Narwhal, Urge*
And *Porpoise*, the last submarine sunk in the war.

OCEAN
Homage to James 'Mick' Magennis VC

At the performance of Merce Cunningham's *Ocean*
In the Waterfront Hall the coral-coloured dancers
Drenched my head with silence and whale messages
And made me feel like a frogman on dry land.

There was room for only one midget submarine
In the roof space where my mind had floated, and where
Swimming from the Falls Road Baths to Singapore
Mick Magennis emerged in his frogman's suit,

Oxygen leaking in telltale bubbles up to heaven,
His expression unfathomable behind the visor
But his modest thumbs-up confirming that, yes,
He had stuck limpet mines on the cruiser *Takao*.

Alongside dog-paddling, ballet-dancing polar bears,
Penguins like torpedoes, dolphins in twos and threes,
Sea otters, seals, Mick was formation-swimming and
At home in the ocean's cupola above my head.

SWEETIE PAPERS
Homage to Pierre Bonnard

When sweeties came back to Mrs Parker's shop we
Drooled over the look of them and smoothed out at home
Tinfoil and cellophane, a little bit like Pierre
Bonnard's collection of sweetie papers, his 'sparkles'
Pinned to the wall, light-conductors for the late
Self-portraits as Japanese soldier or collaborator
Punched and kicked in the face until his eyes close
Or death camp survivor, the skin across his chest
Transparent as cigarette paper, and we gazed
Through the squares as through a stained glass window
And almost understood why the unremembered
People sheltering inside the bombed cathedral
Would linger in the changing light, then disappear
Before the end of the war and the end of rationing.

THE EVENING STAR
in memory of Catherine Mercer, 1994–96

The day we buried your two years and two months
So many crocuses and snowdrops came out for you
I tried to isolate from those galaxies one flower:
A snowdrop appeared in the sky at dayligone,

The evening star, the star in Sappho's epigram
Which brings back everything that shiny daybreak
Scatters, which brings the sheep and brings the goat
And brings the wean back home to her mammy.

BROKEN DISHES

Sydney our mutual friend is kneeling by your bed
Hour after hour on the carpetless hospital floor.
He repeats the same kind words and they become
An invocation to you and you start to die.

You love your body. So does Sydney. So do I.
Communion is blankets and eiderdown and sheets.
All I can think of is a quilt called *Broken Dishes*
And spreading it out on the floor beneath his knees.

THE SNOW LEOPARD
in memory of Fiona Jackson, 1970–95

I

I couldn't recommend to you the Elysian Fields
At the world's end with fair-haired Rhadamanthus,
Though there, Fiona, you would still be you, your body
Temperature controlled by westerlies off the waves,

No snowfall, according to the old man of the sea,
No cold spells or cloudbursts to help you feel at home,
No wreaths of frost flowers on your bedroom window,
No snowman in the garden as your memorial.

II

Let me add mine to all the bouquets wrapped in tinfoil
And tied to the bollard where your car careered
A mile from Sandymount, a mile from where your cat
Curled in and out of our one and only conversation.

III

The snow leopard that vanishes in a whirlwind of snow
Can be seen stalking on soft paws among the clouds.

THE DAFFODILS

Your daughter is reading to you over and over again
Wordsworth's 'The Daffodils', her lips at your ear.
She wants you to know what a good girl you have been.
You are so good at joined-up writing the page you
Have filled with your knowledge is completely black.
Your hand presses her hand in response to rhyme words.
She wants you to turn away from the wooden desk
Before you die, and look out of the classroom window
Where all the available space is filled with daffodils.

THE MUSTARD TIN

You are dying and not sleeping soundly because
Your eyes stay open and it doesn't seem to hurt.
We want you to blink and find three of us standing
For a few seconds between you and the darkness.

Your mouth has opened so wide you appear to scream.
We will need something to close your terrible yawn.
I hoke around in my childhood for objects without
Sharp edges and recover the oval mustard tin.

A daughter strokes your forehead and says: 'There. There.'
A daughter holds your hand and says: 'I'm sorry.'
I focus on the mustard tin propping your jaw,
On the total absence of the oval mustard tin.

THE ALTAR CLOTH
in memory of Marie Ewart

I

You poked your knitting needles through the ball of wool
And laid them beside your glasses on an open book.
You gave the fish in your fish soup a German name.
To begin with you seemed small and elderly to me.

Then you expanded and grew young and beautiful,
Your laughter a wild duck's navigational call,
Your argumentativeness Alexandrian, obstreperous
Your liking for big obstreperous dogs with big tails.

Wherever you are I would have in your vicinity
Wild figs ripening along the bumpiest side-road
And, even if an adder dozes near that carpet,
Masses of cyclamens on the path to the waterfall.

II

In the Piazza Vecchia there are only two houses,
Yours and San Rocco's chapel, so diminutive
It fits like a kennel the saint and the faithful dog
That brings him a loaf of bread daily in the story.

The falling star we saw the night before his festival
May have had nothing to do with his birthmark
Shaped like a cross, or the plague sore on his thigh
He keeps lifting the hem of his tunic to show us,

But, for the split second it managed to stay alight,
The meteor was heading for your household and his
Which is furnished with one table, candlesticks
And shell cases from the last war filled with flowers.

III

Think of San Giorgio's church who takes the dragon on
And leaves hardly any room for the undersized saint
Balancing the altar on his head, custodian,
We agree, of all we love about the Romanesque.

Shouldn't we be sheltering beneath the altar cloth's
Pattern of grapes and vine leaves, for this is our last
Conversation and the crab is nipping your synapses,
Sifting your memory through its claws and frilly lips?

Marie, I only know this in retrospect. Otherwise
I'd have washed your hair and tranquillized your brain
With evening mist that fills the Valle del Serchio and
Lingers at the bottom of the village between the vines.

AN ELEGY
in memory of George Mackay Brown

After thirty years I remember the rusty scythe
That summarised in the thatch the deserted village,

And the anchor painted silver so that between showers
Between Hoy and Stromness it reflected the sunshine.

Now the anchor catches the light on the ocean floor.
The scythe too is gleaming in some underwater room.

MAUREEN MURPHY'S WINDOW

Because you've built shelves across the big window, keep-
Sakes and ornaments become part of the snowy garden.

The footprints we and the animals leave in the snow
Borrow the blue from the blue glassware you collect.

I imagine your dead husband moving in and out
Through window and shelves without breaking a thing.

He is the snow poet and he keeps his snow shoes on.

BJÖRN OLINDER'S PICTURES

I have learned about dying by looking at two pictures
Björn Olinder needed to look at when he was dying:
A girl whose features are obscured by the fall of her hair
Planting a flower,
                and a seascape: beyond the headland
A glimpse of immaculate sand that awaits our footprints.

THE LATECOMERS
for Britta Olinder

One week late for Helena Hallqvist's ninetieth birthday,
We see her for the first time in the *gamla kyrka*.
Sitting at right angles to us, she gazes ahead
At the pulpit and the candles the sun doesn't put out.

She looks up at the ceiling built like a hull, at Christ
Straddling a rainbow that fades into the woodwork.
From just in front of her earlobe three dainty wrinkles
Ripple outwards as crinkles at her daughter's ear.

'The kingdom of heaven is like this,' the pastor begins.
We are the latecomers in his sermon, the labourers
Hired at the eleventh hour and paid an equal wage
To those who bore 'the burden and heat of the day'.

We are not too late for her birthday, who have sweated
For only one hour in the vineyard and earned our penny.

THE SHAKER BARN

I would lie down with you here, side by side,
Our own memorials in what amounts to
The Shakers' cathedral, this circular hay barn,
The two of us fieldmice under storeys of hay,

Tons of hay, a column of hay that changes
The ceiling into a gigantic waggon wheel
Or a rose window made entirely of wood
Which we can see through as far as the sky.

THE HUT

If the hut still existed, I would take you there
To contemplate the waterfall at Glenariff
Through three panes of glass the colour of dawn
And noon and sunset, a cobwebby perspective,

A windy, wide-open snug, a shrine to daylight,
Our time together measured by water falling
And the silence beneath the roar, a pebble
That rotates and dwindles in its rumbling hole.

THE YELLOW TEAPOT

When those who had eaten at our table and drunk
From the yellow teapot into the night, betrayed you
And told lies about you, I cried out for a curse
And wrote a curse, then stitched together this spell,
A quilt of quilt names to keep you warm in the dark:

Snake's Trail, Shoo Fly, Flying Bats, Spider Web,
Broken Handle, Tumbling Blocks, Hole in the Barn
Door, Dove at the Window, Doors and Windows,
Grandmother's Flower Garden, Sun Dial, Mariner's
Compass, Delectable Mountains, World without End.

THE SUNBURST

Her first memory is of light all around her
As she sits among pillows on a patchwork quilt
Made out of uniforms, coat linings, petticoats,
Waistcoats, flannel shirts, ball gowns, by Mother
Or Grandmother, twenty stitches to every inch,
A flawless version of *World without End* or
Cathedral Window or a diamond pattern
That radiates from the smallest grey square
Until the sunburst fades into the calico.

THE DESIGN

Sometimes the quilts were white for weddings, the design
Made up of stitches and the shadows cast by stitches.
And the quilts for funerals? How do you sew the night?

THE QUILT
for Peggy O'Brien

I come here in the dark, I shall leave here in the dark –
No time to look around Amherst and your little house,
To talk of your ill father, my daughter's broken – no,
There isn't time – tears in the quilt, patterns repeating.

And yet as antique orphan and girlish granny we
Stitch a square of colour on the darkness, needle-
Work, material and words, Emily's bedroom window
With a bowl of flowers we pick out through the glass.

An iron bedstead you brought over from Tralee fills up
The box-room where I snooze, as though I have become
For these few hours in February your father, your son,

While in your neighbourhood instead of snow the bushes
Wear quilts left out all night to dry, like one enormous
Patchwork spring-cleaned, well-aired, mended by morning.

FOUND POEM
after Ann Petry

As it developed, Harriet Tubman,
Conductor on the Underground Railroad
Which was really the long road to the North
And emancipation for runaway slaves,
Thought her quilt pattern as beautiful
As the wild flowers that grew in the wood
And along the edges of the roads. The
Yellow was like the Jerusalem flower,
And the purple suggested motherwort,
And the white pieces were like water
Lily, and the varying shades of green
Represented the leaves of all the plants,
And the eternal green of the pine trees.

THE LEVEL CROSSING

The ticks her children and the two dogs bring in from the fields
Are all that's wrong with living here, says the young woman
Who sits beside me. And the spring rains. The bus driver
Worries about hitting deer on the road and recites his recipe
For marinading venison. Plenty of oregano and garlic.

The freight train trundles for ages through the centre of town.
On the other side of the track the endlessness of Illinois
Awaits us, and the sky teetering around a solitary tree.
I forget to ask about the cure for ticks. I want to go home.
A deer's leap in the dark. Patience at the level crossing.

LEAVING ATLANTA

I shall miss my students and the animals – chipmunks
Vanishing into the lawn, on their twiggy trampoline
The squirrels, a raccoon activating the alarm lights,
'He who scratches with his hands', the Indians named him,
And no visitors to the verandah more ghostly than
The lugubrious opossum and her child – my students
And the animals combining underground, overhead,
Wherever the mind goes in the small hours, at sunrise.

THE DIAMOND

In the dungy dusk of Jessica Tyrrell's
Pony's stable in Kildalkey, the diamond
On Rusty's forehead concentrates the light
Like a beacon for nesting house martins
Lost in the roof space, an artistic touch,
A splash of birdlime, a blaze in the brain.

THE BRANCH

The artist in my father transformed the diagonal
Crack across the mirror on our bathroom cabinet
Into a branch: that was his way of mending things,
A streak of brown paint, dabs of green, an accident
That sprouted leaves,

                        awakening the child in me
To the funny faces he pulls when he is shaving.
He wears a vest, white buttons at his collarbone.
The two halves of my father's face are joining up.
His soapy nostrils disappear among the leaves.

PAPER BOATS
Homage to Ian Hamilton Finlay

        fold paper boats
        for the boy Odysseus
        and launch them

        ship-shape
        happy-go-lucky
        in the direction of Troy

SCRAP METAL

I

Helen Denerley made this raven out of old iron,
Belly and back the brake shoes from a lorry, nuts
And bolts for legs and feet, the wings ploughshares
('Ridgers', she elaborates, 'for tatties and neeps'),
The eyeballs cogs from a Morris Minor gearbox.

The bird poses on the circular brass tray my mother
(And now I) polished, swipes of creamy Brasso,
Then those actions, melting a frosty window pane,
Clearing leaves from a neglected well, her breath
Meeting her reflection in the ultimate burnish.

The beak I identified first as a harrow tooth
Is the finger from an old-fashioned finger-bar
Mower for dividing and cutting down the grass,
And, as he bends his head to drink, the raven points
To where the surface gives back my mother's features.

II

The head I pat is made out of brake calipers
With engine mountings from a Toyota for ears,
The spine a baler chain, the ruff and muscular neck
Sprockets, plough points, clutch plate, mower blades,

The legs a Morris Minor kingpin or swingle tree.
Snow in Aberdeenshire and Helen's garden. A wolf
At the forest's edge where scrap metal multiplies
Waits on claw-hammer feet for the rest of the pack.

THE FOX

Where the burn separating Carrigskeewaun
From Thallabaun crosses the path to the cottage
And fencing crosses the water, flood water
Has hung among grass clumps and black plastic
A fox who tries to sidestep death, decay
And barbed wire by foxtrotting upside down
Against the camber of the Milky Way.

THE RABBIT
for Ciaran Carson

I closed my eyes on a white horse pulling a plough
In Poland, on a haystack built around a pole,
And opened them when the young girl and her lover
Took out of a perforated cardboard shoe-box
A grey rabbit, an agreeable shitty smell,
Turds like a broken rosary, the slow train
Rocking this dainty manger scene, so that I
With a priestly forefinger tried to tickle
The narrow brain-space behind dewdrop eyes
And it bounced from her lap and from her shoulder
Kept mouthing 'prunes and prisms' as if to warn
That even with so little to say for itself
A silly rabbit could pick up like a scent trail
My gynaecological concept of the warren
With its entrances and innermost chamber,
Or the heroic survival in Warsaw's sewers
Of just one bunny saved as a pet or meal,
Or its afterlife as *Hasenpfeffer* with cloves
And bay leaves, onions – enough! – and so
It would make its getaway when next I dozed
Crossing the Oder, somewhere in Silesia
(Silesian lettuce, h'm), never to meet again,
Or so I thought, until in Lodz in the small hours
A fat hilarious prostitute let that rabbit bop
Across her shoulders without tousling her hair-do
And burrow under her chin and nuzzle her ear
As though it were crooning 'The Groves of Blarney'
Or 'She Walked Unaware', then in her cleavage
It crouched as in a ploughed furrow, ears laid flat,
Pretending to be a stone, safe from stoat and fox.

THE HARE

Through a grille of rushes and yellowing grass
You watch me come and go at Carrigskeewaun,
Until I loom over your form like Mweelrea,

Your draughty lackadaisical basket still warm,
Still warm the earth that was rough and ready
Even when you were born, your blue eyes open.

You juke and disappear behind the cottage,
Then lollop after me to Lucca and join
Elephant, wild boar, dromedary on the façade.

You leave pawprints in marble and your grassy
Boat-shape with its inch of improvised rigging
Sets sail past the cottage and the cathedral.

LEOPARDI'S SONG THRUSH

Have they eaten all the thrushes here in Italy?
In the resonant Valle del Serchio I have heard
Thunder claps, church bells, the melancholy banter
Of gods and party-goers, echoes from mountaintops
And Alessandro's hillside bar, but not one thrush.

Rather than the missel thrush, the stormcock fluting
Through bad weather on its diet of mistletoe,
I mourn five or six sky-coloured eggs, anvil stones
For tenderising snails, repetitious phrases,
Leopardi's thrush, the song thrush in particular.

My lamentation a batsqueak from the balcony,
I stick some thorns onto the poet's beloved broom
And call it gorse (or whin or furze), a prickly
Sanctuary for the song thrush among yellow flowers,
Its underwing flashing yellow as it disappears.

PASCOLI'S PORTRAIT

Dining under your portrait at Ponte di Campia
I need hardly apologise for not knowing
Your poetry, although I hear wingbeats and see
An eye that sees the skylark and the skylark's eye.

Since a poem's little more than a wing and a prayer,
I turn back to my dinner and pretend our souls
Are roosting on the broken lamp beneath the eaves.
Splashes of birdlime on the pavement give us away.

THE MUSICAL BOX

As well as querulous house martins and the bells
That clang out from San Ginese's to waken up
The terracotta tortoise dozing between the tongs
And the wood stove, and distract the bronze herons,
One listening to the ceiling, the other to the floor,

There is so much music in your house, it contracts
In my mind to a musical box with room enough
For the old woman who ran a kindergarten
In this kitchen – simple addition, tonic solfa –
And for the man who kept canaries under the roof.

ETRURIA

Pavese's English poems, an English setter barking –
Too hot and clammy to read, sleep, dander, so
Snap my walking stick in two and lay it out beside
My long bones in an ossuary that tells a story,

The apprentice ivory carver's yarn, for instance,
Who etched those elderly twinkling Chinese pilgrims
On a walnut, shell-crinkles their only obstacle,
Globe-trotters in my palm, the kernel still rattling.

You can find me under the sellotaped map fold
Stuck with dog hairs, and close to a mulberry bush
The women tended, coddling between their breasts
The silkworms' filaments, vulnerable bobbins.

Was it a humming bird or a humming bird moth
Mistook my navel for some chubby convolvulus?
Paolo steps from his *casa* like an astronaut
And stoops with smoky bellows among his bees.

Gin, acacia honey, last year's sloes, crimson
Slipping its gravity like the satellite that swims
In and out of the hanging hornet-traps, then
Jukes between midnight planes and shooting stars.

The trout that dozed in a perfect circle wear
Prison grey in the fridge, bellies sky-coloured
Next to the butter dish's pattern, traveller's joy,
Old man's beard when it seeds, feathery plumes.

The melon Adua leaves me on the windowsill
Gift-wrapped in a paper bag and moonlight,
Ripens in moon-breezes, the pipistrelles' whooshes,
My own breathing and the insomniac aspen's.

A liver concocted out of darkness and wine
Dregs, the vinegar mother sulking in her crock
Haruspicates fever, shrivelled grapes, vipers
On the footpath to a non-existent waterfall.

I escape the amorous mongrel with dewclaws
And vanish where once the privy stood, my kaftan
Snagging on the spiral staircase down to the small
Hours when house and I get into bed together,

My mattress on the floor, crickets, scorpion shapes
In their moonlit square, my space in this cellar
Beneath old rafters and old stones, Etruria,
Nightmare's cesspit, the mosquito-buzz of sleep.

THE BLACKTHORN

A bouquet for my fifties, these flowers without leaves
Like easter snow, hailstones clustering at dayligone –
From the difficult thicket a walking stick in bloom, then
Astringency, the blackthorn and its smoky plum.

FRAGMENT
after Attila József

Forty years I've been at it, working hard,
A poetic pro, no longer the neophyte.
I'm standing near the metalworker's yard
And can't find the words for this starry night.

REMEMBERING THE POETS

As a teenage poet I idolised the poets, doddery
Macer trying out his *Ornithogonia* on me,
And the other one about herbal cures for snake bites,
Propertius, my soul mate, love's polysyllabic
Pyrotechnical laureate reciting reams by heart,
Ponticus straining to write The Long Poem, Bassus
(Sorry for dropping names) iambic to a fault,
Horace hypnotising me with songs on the guitar,
Virgil, our homespun internationalist, sighted
At some government reception, and then Albius
Tibullus strolling in the woods a little while
With me before he died, his two slim volumes
An echo from the past, a melodious complaint
That reaches me here, the last of the singing line.

THE BEECH TREE

Leaning back like a lover against this beech tree's
Two-hundred-year-old pewter trunk, I look up
Through skylights into the leafy cumulus, and join
Everybody who has teetered where these huge roots
Spread far and wide our motionless mossy dance,
As though I'd begun my eclogues with a beech
As Virgil does, the brown envelopes unfolding
Like fans their transparent downy leaves, tassels
And prickly cups, mast, a fall of vermilion
And copper and gold, then room in the branches
For the full moon and her dusty lakes, winter
And the poet who recollects his younger self
And improvises a last line for the georgics
About snoozing under this beech tree's canopy.

THE GARDEN

When Nausicaa described to Odysseus how her mother
Would sit at the hearth as a rule and embroider by firelight
A delightful picture with yarn the colour of sea-purple,
Her chair against a pillar, the maidservants seated behind
And her father up on his throne sipping wine like a god,
Was she proposing what he would later find out for himself
In the spacious garden, four acres surrounded by fences,
Where the trees grow tall and leafy, pear and pomegranate,
Apple with its shiny crop, sweet fig and opulent olive,
Fruit that never runs out, summer or winter, all year
The breathy west wind germinating and ripening apple
After apple, pear after pear, grape cluster on grape cluster,
Fig upon fig; in a sun-trap the sun sun-drying grapes
While others are picked for eating or the wine press, nearby
Green bunches casting their blossom or darkening a little,
And the well-ordered vegetable plots, herbs, perennials,
The whole garden irrigated by one spring, another
Gushing under the haggard gate to supply the big house?

BIRDS & FLOWERS
for Fuyuji Tanigawa

My local The Chelsea where I took you for a pint
Has been demolished, which leaves us drinking in the rain,
Two inky smiles on handkerchiefs tied for luck like dolls
Flapping where the window should be, in Ireland or Japan.

A wagtail pauses among maple leaves turning from red
To pink in the picture you enclose with your good news:
'I have been a man of home these years,' you write, 'often
Surprised to know so much passion hidden in myself.'

You who translated for me 'ichigo-ichie' as 'one life,
One meeting' as though each encounter were once-in-a-
Lifetime, have been spending time with your little children:
'But I will go back to the world of letters soon.' Fuyuji,

The world of letters is a treacherous place. We are weak
And unstable. Let us float naked again in volcanic
Pools under the constellations and talk about babies.
The picture you sent to Belfast is called 'Birds & Flowers'.

THE WATERFALL

If you were to read my poems, all of them, I mean,
My life's work, at the one sitting, in the one place,
Let it be here by this half-hearted waterfall
That allows each pebbly basin its separate say,
Damp stones and syllables, then, as it grows dark
And you go home past overgrown vineyards and
Chestnut trees, suppliers once of crossbeams, moon–
Shaped nuts, flour, and crackly stuffing for mattresses,
Leave them here, on the page, in your mind's eye, lit
Like the fireflies at the waterfall, a wall of stars.

INVOCATION

Begin the invocation: rice cakes, say, buckwheat
Flowers or temple bells, bamboo, a caged cricket
Cheeping for the girl who plants the last rice seed.
I have a good idea of what's going on outside.

NOTES & ACKNOWLEDGEMENTS

Several of the war poems owe a great deal to my friend Jane Leonard's researches into the First World War and its memorials. 'Found Poem' versifies a passage from *Harriet Tubman, Conductor on the Underground Railway*, by Ann Petry (HarperCollins, New York, 1955). 'Poetry' is based on episodes from *Edmund Blunden* by Barry Webb (Yale University Press, 1990). 'Death of a Horse' is derived from Keith Douglas's short story of that name which is included in *A Prose Miscellany*, ed. Desmond Graham (Carcanet Press, 1985).

Under the title *Broken Dishes* seventeen poems were published as a chapbook by Abbey Press (Newry) in April 1998. Abbey Press also published in October 1999 *Out of the Cold* which combined drawings by Sarah Longley with some of these poems. Fifteen poems made up a programme called *Cenotaph of Snow* which was produced by Tim Dee and broadcast on BBC Radio 4 in August 1998.

'Leopardi's Song Thrush' was written specially for *At the Year's Turning*, ed. Marco Sonzogni (Dedalus Press); 'The Factory' for *A Tribute to Brendan Kennelly*, ed. Äke Persson (Bloodaxe Books); and 'The Beech Tree' for the Salisbury *Last Words* Festival.

Acknowledgements are due to the following publications: *Agenda, Black Mountain Review, Brangle, Chapman, Chicago Review, College Green, Irish Recorder, Irish Review, Irish Times, London Review of Books, Metre, New Hibernia Review, New Yorker, Observer, Poetry Ireland Review, Poetry Review, Princeton Library Review, Sappho Through the Ages, Signals, Thumbscrew*, and to the BBC and RTE.

I use several Scots (or Ulster Scots) words, three of which may require a gloss: *hurly-gush* (p. 9) means a noisy rush of water; *peerie-heedit* (p. 13) means 'with a spinning top for a head', confused, disorientated; *dayligone* (pp. 29 & 54) means twilight, dusk.